BLS For Healthcare Providers Student Manual

Basic Life Support Handbook

Jane John-Nwankwo RN, MSN

BLS FOR HEALTHCARE PROVIDERS STUDENT MANUAL:
Basic Life Support Handbook

ISBN-13: 978-1497343122

ISBN-10: 1497343127

Printed in the United States of America.

Dedication

To my loving husband, John U. Nwankwo Ph.D

OTHER TITLES FROM THE SAME AUTHOR:

1. **Work At Home Jobs For Nurses & Other Healthcare Professionals**
2. **Nurses' Romance Series**
3. **CNA Exam Prep: Nurse Assistant Practice Test Questions. Vol. One and Two**
4. **Patient Care Technician Exam Review Questions: PCT Test Prep**
5. **IV Therapy & Blood Withdrawal Review Questions**
6. **Medical Assistant Test Preparation**
7. **EKG Test Prep**
8. **Phlebotomy Test Prep Vol 1, 2, & 3**
9. **The Home Health Aide Textbook**
10. **How to make a million in nursing**

And Many More Books

Visit www.healthcarepracticetest.com

The goal of CPR is to save lives. Compressions must be started within 10 seconds of cardiac arrest

Since its introduction to American physicians in 1960, CPR has remained a staple of emergency medicine. More people continue to be trained in CPR administration not only in America but other countries in order to save lives. In the recent times, the American Heart Association introduced the 'hands-only CPR' whereby rescue forgo rescue breaths. Despite the advancements made, the effectiveness of the CPR is still low in the country. To address the challenge there are calls to introduce CPR training in schools and increase access to automated external defibrillators. This study guide examines the key CPR concepts.

What is Cardio-Pulmonary Resuscitation?

Cardio Pulmonary Resuscitation is an emergency procedure that is performed to restore spontaneous blood circulation and breathing in the victims. The practice encompasses core components such as airway control, artificial respiration and cardiac massage. According to Mistovich and Karren (2010) Vesalius is credited with the earliest account of artificial respiration and airway control. Later on, Tossach conducted the first documented resuscitation on an injured coal miner. These early pioneers popularized the concept of mouth-to-mouth resuscitation but it was later disregarded due to hygienic reasons. Later on in 1800s, Leroy d'Etiolles introduced the idea of manipulating the body to induce ventilation. In 1958, Safar, Escarraga and Elam published an article which saw the re-introduction of the mouth-to-mouth resuscitation (Safar, 1989). Their findings were supported by the National Research Council of the National Academy of Sciences. The 1800s saw the introduction of the cardiac massage. Early in the 20th century, George Washington Crile wrote an article to popularize the combination of the thoracic compression, artificial respiration and parenteral epinephrine infusion.

The CPR process is used to re-start a patient's heart after it has stopped pumping. The main essence of CPR is to continue to pump blood to vital organs, especially the brain to prevent brain death which usually occurs in few minutes without oxygen (which of course the blood supplies). According to Huether and McCance (2004) heart failure may be caused by many factors including unhealthy lifestyle, heart-related illnesses, accidents and chronic diseases. According to the available literature, CPR has been effective in patients who suffered from heart attack secondary to severe kidney failure, cancer, severe heart failure and serious infection. However, CPR is associated with various side effects. For instance, pushing down the rib bones may cause further injury to the victims and secondly, CPR can puncture the lungs or cause damage to the other organs in the thoracic cavity.

Why do we have to do CPR?

The CPR process is very important to the victim and is composed of several functions. The first function is neutralizing any dangers from the surroundings. The rescuer should ensure any hazards are removed and the victims are well taken care of. The second component is checking the status of the victim by asking questions and if the victim does not respond the rescuer should send for help. The third component is unblocking the airway and checking for breathing. After checking for breathing, the rescuer is then supposed to start the compressions. According to Mistovich and Karren (2010) the rescuer should first administer 30 compressions at a rate of 2 compressions per second. All along, the rescuer should make sure the victims are lying on their backs and the head and the chin is lifted. The CPR should be repeated in a cycle of 30 compressions and 2 rescue breaths. If the victim fails to respond to the CPR, an automated external defibrillator should be used. It is very paramount that chest compressions be started immediately, not more than 10 seconds from the time of cardiac arrest. If you don't feel a pulse, or are not sure you feel a pulse, start chest compressions!

According to Mistovich and Karren (2010) chest compressions during CPR generate small but critical amount of blood flow to the heart and brain. Mistovich and Karren (2010) further suggest that the quality of the chest compressions determines the success of the resuscitation. The physiology of chest compressions can be understood using the external; cardiac massage and thoracic pump models. According to Huether and McCance (2004), external cardiac massage compresses the cardiac structures hence forcing the blood to circulate. On the other hand, the thoracic pump model suggests that chest compressions increase the global intra-thoracic pressure. During the CPR process the brain is susceptible to the decreased blood flow and could suffer from irreversible damage within five minutes of absent perfusion. Chest compressions ensure blood circulates to the brains and other susceptible organs such as the myocardium (the muscles of the heart).

The appropriate way to do compressions

Given the importance of the chest compressions, it is important that the rescuer administers them in the right manner. Chest compressions are supposed to be forceful and should be administered on the lower half of the sternum. The victim should be placed in a supine position while the rescuer kneels beside the victim's chest. For compressive force to be effective, the patients should be placed in a firm surface. In addition, interruptions of chest compressions should be avoided and the rescuer should take maximum care not to dislodge lines and tubes. The rescuer should place the dominant hand on the center of the victim's chest. The heel of his or her hands should be positioned in the midline and aligned with the long axis of the sternum. The non-dominant hand should be placed over the dominant one, with the fingers elevated off the patient's ribs. This arrangement ensures the rescuer is able to apply enough

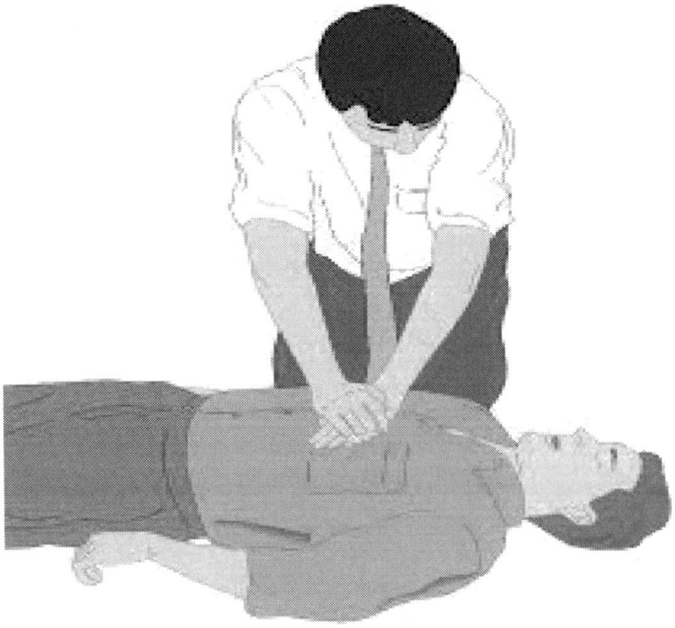

compressive force and to minimize damage of the ribs. The rescuer should avoid applying force over the xiphisternum (tip of the sternum) and the upper abdomen. While applying pressure on the victim's chest, the rescuer should keep his arms straight and extended. The rescuer's shoulders should be positioned vertically above the victim's chest to ensure maximize the effectiveness of the compressive forces. In the article titled, *technique for chest compressions in adult CPR*, Rajab, Conrad, Cohn and Schmitto (2011) suggests that chest compressions should be delivered at a rate of at least 100 per minute and any interruptions should be avoided. In the same article, Rajab, Conrad, Cohn and Schmitto (2011) argue that compression depth should be maintained at 5 cm and the rescuer should allow the victim's chest to recoil completely. In addition, the rescuer should avoid removing his or her hands from the victim's chest, in order to maintain the right compression depth. The rescuer should observe a duty cycle of 50% and the compressor should be rotated every two minutes. Chest compression is terminated after the patient recovers or when the Emergency Response Team arrives to continue ACLS (Advanced Cardio Vascular Life Support).

The BLS Survey

The American Heart Association recommends training of persons to equip them with the necessary skills to save lives. Receiving the CPR training gives the rescuers the ability to perform basic activities such as restoring the blood circulation, clearing the airway, and conducting rescue breathing. One of the major components of the BLS survey is checking the responsiveness of the patient by tapping or shouting. The rescuer is also supposed to determine whether the patient is breathing or not. To determine whether the patient is breathing or not, the rescuer should listen for breath sounds. Alternatively, the rescuer should use the cheeks to feel the flow of air from the patient's breaths. The next key component of the BLS survey is activating the emergency response system and obtaining an automated external defibrillator (AED). According to the acceptable principles, the rescuer is required to activate the Emergency Response System and begin the CPR after establishing that the patient is unresolved and is unable to breathe. Another key step is checking for the carotid pulses. If the patient is unresponsive or if he or she is not breathing well, the rescuer should take not more than 10 seconds in checking for a pulse. In the absence of a pulse, chest compressions should be administered immediately. As suggested by the 2010s, AHA guidelines for CPR and ECC, the rescuer should adhere to the C-A-B sequence (Compressions-Airway-Breathing). The last component of the BLS survey is defibrillation. A defibrillator or AED is used to check for a shockable rhythm and is normally used in the absence of a pulse.

Pocket masks

As earlier indicated, mouth-to-mouth resuscitation is the cornerstone of the CPR. However, there is reluctance by the medical professionals to use this type of resuscitation. One of the common reasons given by nurses and the physicians is the fear of contracting diseases and infections. Their observations are supported by a study conducted by Handley (2002) which shows that HIV transmission can occur due to trauma, oral lesions and contact with blood. It is for this reason, that the medical practitioners are advised to carry pocket masks. Pocket masks are considered to be effective in delivering rescue breaths to the patient during cardiac or respiratory arrest. The pocket masks have a pre-inflated cuff to provide an effective seal around the mouth and the nose. The one-way valve reduce contamination while the in-line filter, filters the air. A pocket mask also has an oxygen inlet port to deliver high-flow oxygen to the patient. The pocket mask is placed on the patient's face with the base of the mask resting between the casualty's chin and the lower lip. The masks are re-usable but the filters and the valve should be discarded after use. According to Handley (2002) the masks are preferred as they create a comfortable distance between the patient and the rescuer. The device also allows the rescuer to observe the chest movements and monitor the patient.

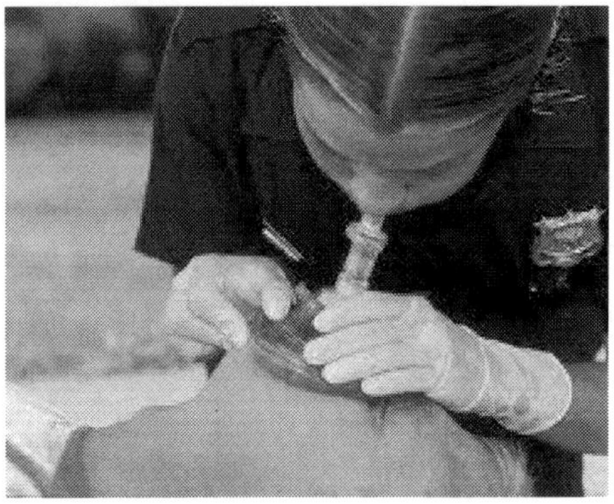

However, while pocket masks are preferred by the medical practitioners, a study conducted by Adelborg et al (2011) indicates that mouth-to-mouth ventilation is superior to mouth-to-pocket masks. In this study, Adelborg et al (2011) used a sample of 60 life guards to perform three sessions of single rescuer CPR. According to Adelborg et al (2011) significantly more ventilation were delivered by the mouth-to-mouth ventilations compared to the mouth-to-pocket masks. But for safety and healthcare reasons, Mouth to mask breathing is resorted to.

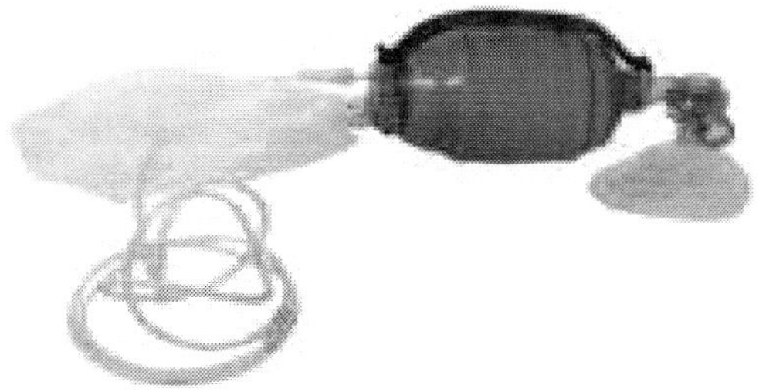

Using the bag mask This device provides positive pressure ventilation to the patients, and made up of a bag and valve combinations. Bag masks have proved to be effective in airway management and providing patients with enough air. Bag masks come in different sizes and are the responsibility of the rescuers to choose the most appropriate one. Bag masks are either attached to the oxygen tank or draw room air. The device is operated by one whereby the rescuer hold holds the BVM with one hand, while the other hand compresses the bag delivering the oxygen. The two-person bag ventilation mask has been shown to be more effective than a singly-operated bag mask in delivering greater tidal volumes and introducing less air leak. When using a bag mask, one is required to position himself or herself above the victim's head. The rescuer then places the mask on the victim's head and holds it in position using the E-C device. Once the mask is in place, the rescuer is then required to press the bag and watch for the chest rise. 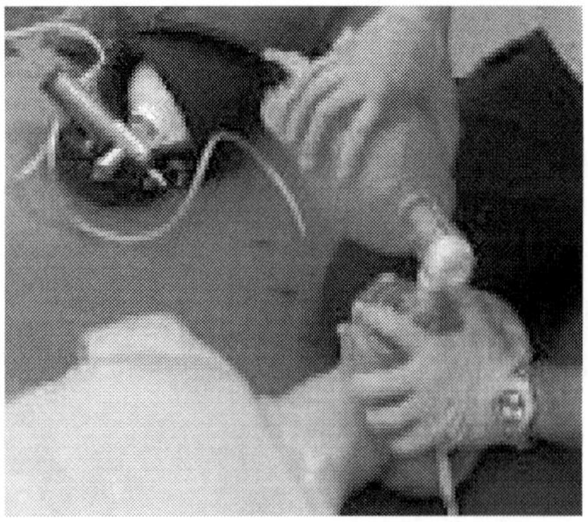

One rescuer CPR and 2 rescuers CPR

There are two basic ways of performing CPR: 1-person CPR and the 2-person CPR. Of the two techniques, the 2-Person CPR is the best, as the victim is able to receive enough air volume and is less tiring. One of the rescuers administers the chest compressions while the other performs the rescue breaths. Alternatively, the two rescuers can switch about every two minutes.

Adult CPR and Child CPR and Infant CPR

In all the patients, the chest compression rate and the sequence is the same: At least 100 compressions per minute. In addition, during the CPR, chest wall recoil should be allowed between compressions and interruption should be limited to less than 10 seconds. The way CPR is administered varies according to the age. The CPR procedure varies among the adults, children and the infants and these differences are shown in the table below.

CPR COMPONENT	**ADULTS**	**CHILDREN**	**INFANTS**
Activating EMS and getting an AED	Call for help and if alone phone EMS immediately	Call for help but if alone, phone EMS after giving 5 cycles of CPR	Call for help but if alone, phone EMS after giving 5 cycles of CPR
COMPRESSION DEPTH	5CM	5CM	4CM
COMPRESSION-VENTILATION RATIO	30:2 1 or 2 rescuers	30:2 Single rescuer 15:2 2 rescuers	30:2 Single rescuer 15:2 2 rescuers
Compression location	Centre of chest	Centre of chest	Just below nipple line on breast bone
Compression method	2hands : heel of 1 hand , other hand on top	1 hand. Or 2 hands if the child is obese. heel of 1 hand , other hand on top	2 fingers: middle and ring or 2 thumbs

While the above shows the differences in CPR entities there are a number of CPR components that are common among the adults, children and the infants. One such component is the type of the response. It is the role of the rescuer to ensure that the environment is safe enough and to establish if the victim is responsive or not. To check for breathing and open the airway, the rescuer is required to tilt the chin and should not take more than five minutes to check for the visual cues such as chest rise. Compression rate in adults, children and the infants should be maintained at a rate of at least 100 compressions per minute while the compression ventilation ration should be held at 30:2. However, for the drowning patients, CPR sequence should start with 2 initiation breaths before chest compressions.

Rescue breathing

Although some of the instructors may not emphasize on rescue breathing, it is considered important in resuscitating the patients. Two breaths are administered for every 30 chest compressions. To breathe air into the patient, the rescuer pinches his or her nose and the closes on the victim's mouth. The rescuer breathes slowly into the victim leading to the rising of the chest. However, a study conducted by Rea et al (2010) insists that there is no need of rescue breathing if the rescuers are not competent enough. These findings are captured in a randomized trial where 981 of the participants received chest compression only while 960 received chest compression plus rescue breathing. In the end Rea et al (2010) concluded that administering chest compressions alone especially in cancer patients increases the overall survival rate.

Choking for an infant

Choking is very common in small children and is caused by swallowing of huge chunks of food. Some of the other objects that small children choke on include: buttons, carrots and toys. Symptoms of choking in children include high pitched breathing, coughing, color changes and lack of breathing. Choking in infants is treated using back slaps and chest thrusts. To administer the back slaps the baby is supported using one hand, facing upside down. The baby is placed on the laps and the back slaps are then administered using the heel of hand. On the other hand, chest thrusts are administered with the baby facing up. The chest thrusts are applied using two fingers just below the nipple line. So, five chest thrusts, then five back slaps (One cycle). Five cycles must be done. After the fifth cycle, the infant's mouth is opened to see if the object has become visible. If the object has become visible, it is carefully removed. Blind sweeping should never be attempted. If it is not visible, continue the back slaps and chest thrusts until help arrives. If chest becomes unresponsive, commence CPR.

Choking for an adult

Choking in adults occurs when foods and other solids partially or completely block the airway. According to the available statistics, choking is a leading case of home injury death in the United States and adults are at an increased risk of choking due to dental problems and age-related illness.

Other causes of choking include:

- eating too fast

- talking with food in the mouth

-wearing dentures and eating foods with wrong texture.

Symptoms of choking include:

-inability to talk, coughing, fainting and clutching of both hands to the throat, usually referred to the universal choking sign.

In adults and children choking is treated using back blows and abdominal thrusts. Blows and thrusts are administered until the obstruction is dislodged. To apply the blows, the victim is made to bend until he or she is near parallel to the ground. The victim is supported with one arm and then the back blows are administered between the shoulder blades. Alternatively, abdominal thrusts should be given, or chest thrusts if the individual is pregnant.

Conclusion

CPR is an important component of emergency response and leads to significant survival rates of the patients. Despite its success some of the procedures are still archaic and infringe on the rights of the rescuers. For this reason, there is need to address some of the concerns raised by the medical practitioners and conduct extensive research in order to simplify the entire process. The best thing one can do for an unresponsive individual is to start chest compressions before help arrives. THAT SINGLE ACT CAN SAVE THE VICTIM'S LIFE!!!

References

Adelborg, K., Dalqas, C., Grove, E., Jorqensen, C., Al-Mashhadi, R. & Lofqren, B. (2011). Mouth-to-mouth ventilation is superior to mouth-to-pocket mask and bag-valve mask ventilation during lifeguard CPR: a randomized study. *Resuscitation*, 82(5), 618-622

Handley, A. J. (2002). Teaching hand placement for chest compression--a simpler technique. RESUSCITATION, 53(1), 29-36

Huether, S., & McCance, K. L. (2004). *Understanding pathophysiology*. St Louis: Mosby

Mistovich, J. J., & Karren, K. J. (2010). *Pre-hospital emergency care.* New Jersey: Pearson education

Rajab, T., Pozner, C., Conrad, C., Cohn, L. & Schmitto, J. (2011). Technique for chest compressions in adult CPR. *World Journal of Emergency Surgery*, 6, 41

Safar, P. (1989). Initiation of closed-chest cardiopulmonary resuscitation basic life support. A personal history. *Resuscitation*, 18, 7–20.

Review Questions

1. What does CPR stand for?
   a. Cardio Precision Rescue
   b. Cardio Pulmonary Resuscitation
   c. Critical Pulmonary Resuscitation
   d. Critical Precision Resuscitation

2. What is the purpose of CPR?
   a. To restore spontaneous blood circulation only
   b. To restore spontaneous breathing
   c. To restore spontaneous blood circulation and breathing
   d. To restore consciousness

3. What is the main essence of CPR?
   a. To provide oxygen to the lungs via mouth to mouth
   b. To provide blood to the lungs to transport oxygen
   c. To provide electrical stimulation to the heart
   d. To continue to pump blood to the vital organs and the brain

4. Which of the following may be a side effect of CPR?
   a. CPR may break ribs and puncture the lungs or other thoracic organs
   b. CPR may cause a head wound
   c. CPR may cause a head wound and bruise the ribs
   d. All of the above

5. The first step in CPR is to:
   a. Start chest compressions
   b. Start with rescue breaths
   c. Unblock the airways

d. Neutralize any dangers from the surroundings

6. After the first step is accomplished you should:
   a. Start chest compressions
   b. Start rescue breaths
   c. Check the victim for responsiveness
   d. None of the above

7. How long can the brain survive without oxygen?
   a. A few hours
   b. A few minutes
   c. A few days
   d. none of theabove

8. Which aspect of CPR determines the success of resuscitation?
   a. Quality of chest compressions
   b. Number of rescue breaths
   c. Speed of CPR
   d. The muscle tone of the person providing CPR

9. The brain could suffer damage from decreased blood flow in how many minutes?
   a. 3 minutes
   b. 5 minutes
   c. 7 minutes
   d. 10minutes

10. Where should compressions be administered on the body?
    a. On the upper half of the sternum
    b. On the abdomen
    c. On the lower half of the sternum
    d. On the collar bone

11. The non-dominant hand should be placed:
    a. In the middle of the sternum with fingers on the ribs

b. Over the dominant hand with fingers elevated off of the ribs
c. Under the dominant hand with fingers elevated off of the ribs
d. On the upper half of the sternum

12. The rescuer should avoid applying force on the:
   a. Upper abdomen
   b. The xiphisternum
   c. The lower sternum
   d. A and B only

13. How many compressions should you perform per minute?
   a. 50
   b. 75
   c. 100
   d. None of the above

14. Compressors should be switched out:
   a. Every 30 seconds
   b. Every 2 minutes
   c. Every minute
   d. Every 5 minutes

15. Compression depth should be:
   a. 2 cm
   b. 5 cm
   c. 7 cm
   d. 1 inch

16. The chest should:
   a. Recoil completely during compressions
   b. Not recoil during compressions
   c. Recoil halfway during compressions
   d. None of the above

17. When should compressions be terminated?
    a. Never
    b. After 2 minutes of compressions
    c. After the patient recovers
    d. After 3 minutes

18. In order to find out if the patient is breathing you should:
    a. Ask the patient if he/she is breathing
    b. Listen or feel for breathing
    c. Ask a bystander if the patient is breathing
    d. Check the AED readout

19. Which of the following is involved in CPR?
    a. Clearing the airway
    b. Restoring blood circulation
    c. Conducting rescue breathing
    d. All of the above

20. How long should you take to check for a pulse?
    a. Not more than 10 seconds
    b. 15 seconds
    c. Not more than 20 seconds
    d. None of the above

21. What is the last component of the BLS survey?
    a. Chest compressions
    b. Rescue breathing
    c. Defibrillation
    d. Tapping and shouting

22. When is a defibrillator used?
    a. Absence of breath
    b. Absence of pulse
    c. Absence of consciousness

d. Absence of the soul

23. Which of the following is a reason that people are sometimes hesitant to perform mouth to mouth?
    a. Possibility of saliva swapping
    b. Possibility of vomit
    c. Possibility of contracting a disease
    d. Possibility of being caught by a spouse

24. What are medical professionals advised to do in order to prevent contracting a disease?
    a. Never perform CPR
    b. Carry and use a pocket mask
    c. Teach someone else to do CPR
    d. None of the above

25. Which of the following are characteristics of a pocket mask?
    a. Pre-inflated cuff to provide a seal around the mouth and nose
    b. One way valve to prevent contamination
    c. An in-line filter to filter the air
    d. All of the above

26. Which of the following statements are true?
    a. The mask is not reusable
    b. The mask is reusable, but must be sterilized
    c. The mask is reusable, but the filter and valve should be discarded after use
    d. The filter and valve are reusable, but the rest of the mask is not

27. Which of the following statements are true?
    a. Studies suggest that masks are just as effective as mouth to mouth
    b. Studies suggest that mouth to mouth is still superior to masks
    c. Studies suggest that masks are superior to mouth to mouth
    d. Studies suggest that letting someone else do mouth to mouth is most effective

28. Which is the best way to perform CPR?
   a. Two people performing CPR
   b. One person performing CPR
   c. Using a defibrillator
   d. Any of the above

29. If you are alone with a child or infant who needs CPR, when should you call for help?
   a. Before beginning CPR
   b. After giving 5 full cycles of CPR
   c. After giving 10 full cycles of CPR
   d. After 1 full cycle of CPR

30. How should you administer CPR to an infant?
   a. With two hands
   b. With one hand
   c. With two fingers
   d. None of the above

31. How should you administer CPR to an average sized child?
   a. With two hands
   b. With one hands
   c. With two fingers
   d. None of the above

32. In drowning patients, CPR should begin with:
   a. Chest compressions
   b. Defibrillation
   c. Two rescue breaths
   d. None of the above

33. How often should a rescue breath be administered?
   a. Two breaths for every thirty compressions
   b. One breath for every 15 compressions

c. Three breaths for every five compressions
d. Two breaths for every 50 compressions

34. Which of the following is a symptom of choking?
a. High pitched breathing
b. coughing
c. Color changes
d. All of the above

35. How is a choking infant treated?
a. The Heimlich maneuver
b. CPR
c. Back slaps and chest compressions
d. All of the above

36. After five cycles of treating a choking infant you should:
a. Blind sweep of the back of the throat
b. Look into the mouth to see if the object is visible
c. Use tweezers to attempt to find the object
d. Use a stick to attempt to dislodge the object

37. How is choking treated in children and adults?
a. Back blows and abdominal thrusts
b. Back blows only
c. Turn the person upside down to dislodge the object
d. CPR

38. Which of the following is a sign of choking amongst adults?
a. Inability to talk
b. Clutching the throat
c. Coughing or fainting
d. All of the above

39. When does choking occur?

a. When breathing stops for unknown reasons
b. When blood circulation stops for unknown reasons
c. When an object completely or partially blocks the airway
d. When the brain ceases to function

40. If a choking victim is pregnant one should:

a. Perform abdominal thrusts
b. Perform mouth to mouth
c. Perform CPR
d. Perform chest thrusts

Answer Key

1. B
2. C
3. D
4. A
5. D
6. C
7. B
8. A
9. B
10. C
11. B
12. D
13. C
14. B
15. B
16. A
17. C
18. B
19. D
20. A
21. C

22.B
23.C
24.B
25.D
26.C
27.B
28.A
29.B
30.C
31.B
32.C
33.A
34.D
35.C
36.B
37.A
38.D
39.C
40.D

OTHER TITLES FROM THE SAME AUTHOR:

1. Work At Home Jobs For Nurses & Other Healthcare Professionals
2. Nurses' Romance Series
3. CNA Exam Prep: Nurse Assistant Practice Test Questions. Vol. One and Two
4. Patient Care Technician Exam Review Questions: PCT Test Prep
5. ACLS Provider Manual
6. Medical Assistant Test Preparation
7. EKG Test Prep
8. Phlebotomy Test Prep Vol 1, 2, & 3
9. The Home Health Aide Textbook
10. How to make a million in nursing

And Many More Books

Visit www.healthcarepracticetest.com

Work At Home
Jobs For Nurses
And Other Healthcare
Professionals
Jane John-Nwankwo, RN

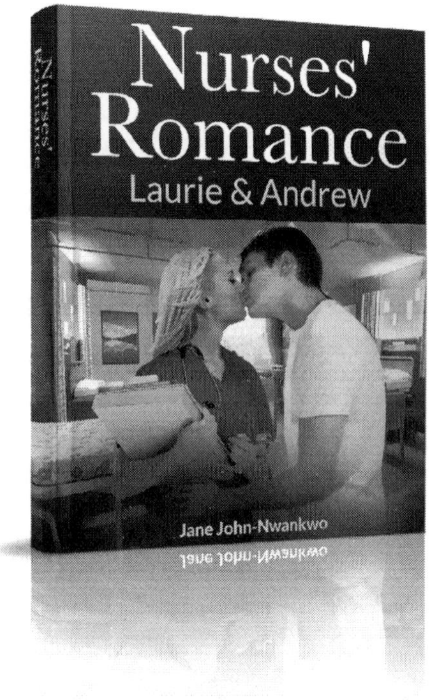
Nurses'
Romance
Laurie & Andrew
Jane John-Nwankwo

The Home Health Aide Textbook
Home Care Principles
Jane John-Nwankwo
RN, MSN

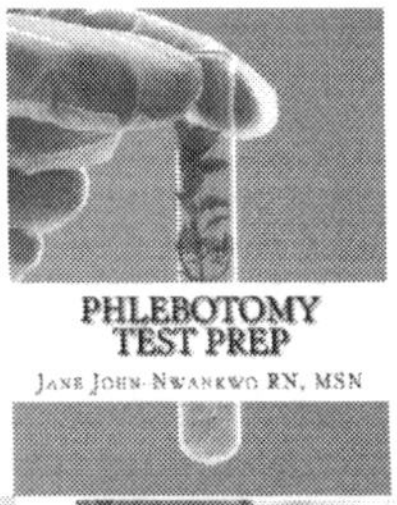
PHLEBOTOMY
TEST PREP
Jane John-Nwankwo RN, MSN

CNA EXAM PREP
Jane John-Nwankwo RN, MSN

EKG TEST
PREP
EKG Technician Exam
Practice Test Questions
JANE JOHN-
NWANKWO RN, MSN

Crisis Prevention
& Intervention
in Healthcare

IV THERAPY AND
BLOOD WITHDRAWAL
REVIEW QUESTIONS
Jane John-Nwankwo RN, MSN

CNA EXAM PREP

43089792R00022

Made in the USA
Lexington, KY
17 July 2015